PROBLEM SOLVING SKILLS
FOR CHILDREN AGES 5-10

Jennifer Leigh Youngs
and Kendahl Brooke Youngs

KENDAHL
HOUSE
PRESS

Kendahl House Press is an imprint of Bettie Youngs Books. If you are unable to order this book from your local bookseller, or online from *Amazon* or *Barnes & Noble*, or from *Espresso*, or from wholesaler *Baker & Taylor*, you may order directly from the publisher: Sales@BettieYoungs.com.

BETTIE YOUNGS BOOK PUBLISHERS / KENDAHL HOUSE PRESS / BURRES BOOKS
www.BettieYoungsBooks.com
info@BettieYoungsBooks.com

Trade Paper ISBN: 978-1-940784-06-9
eBook ISBN: 978-1-940784-05-2

Library of Congress Control Number: 2014947375

1. Kendahl House Press. 2. Bettie Youngs Books. 3. Problem Solving. 4. Problem Solving Skills. 5. Children. 6. Family. 7. Self-Esteem. 8. Happiness. 9. Problem Resolution. 10. Anger Management. 11. Self-Image. 12. Jennifer L. Youngs. 13. Kendahl B. Youngs. 14. Bullying. 15. Childhood Behavior.

Contents

PART I: The 5-Step Process to Solving Problems.................................. 1
  *What is the problem?
  *How can I solve it?
  *What is my plan?
  *When will I do this?
  *How did my plan work?
  Help Josh Solve His Problem
  Help Susan Solve Her Problem
  Help Carlos Solve His Problem
  Help Serena Solve Her Problem
  Your Turn To Solve Problems of Your Own

PART II: Don't Make a Problem Bigger Than It Is................................. 13
  Help Tyrone Solve His Problem
  Help Maria Solve Her Problem
  Help Edward Solve His Problem
  Help Brad Solve His Problem
  Your Turn To Solve Problems of Your Own

PART III: Other Things You Can Do That Make it Easier To Solve
Problems 25
  Express Yourself
  Being Your Own "Best Friend"
  Good Self-Esteem Helps You Be, and Do, Better
  Sharing Happiness
  Sharing Positive Feelings
  Who is Your "Help! Team"?

Eat Foods That Are Good For You
Exercise Is Important to Thinking Clearly
Good Ways to Relax

Other Books by Kendahl House Press and
Bettie Youngs Book Publishers 41

PART I

THE 5-STEP PROCESS TO SOLVING PROBLEMS

From time to time, everyone has problems of one kind or another. The good news is that most problems can be solved. If you stop and think before you take action, you might even be able to prevent the problem from getting bigger.

In this book, you will learn some positive ways to deal with problems. Making the situation better begins by asking yourself these five questions:

* What is the problem?
* How can I solve it?
* What is my plan?
* When will I do this?
* How did my plan work?

Asking these questions will help you find the best solution

to many different kinds of problems. Let's talk about this a little more.

1. What is the problem?

Ask yourself, "What is the problem?" Let's say a friend has said something that hurt your feelings. That can be a problem, and the next step is to decide what you are going to do about it.

But before you do anything, tell your mom or dad or teacher about the problem, because not all problems can be solved by you alone. Sometimes you need a little help.

2. How can I solve it?

There are many ways to solve a problem. Before you decide what you are going to do about a problem you have, think of all the ways you could solve this problem. The more ways you can think of, the better. As you do this, don't worry whether or not the idea would make the problem go away. In fact, some of your ideas may be a little silly and not such a good idea, such as dumping a bowl of spaghetti over your friend's head!

Some ideas might be the wrong thing to do—such as hitting the person. Some ideas might be good—like trying to talk with that person about the problem, but maybe you feel like you are unable to go through with it. For now, at this stage of solving the problem, think of ALL the things you could do to solve the problem. And, don't forget to tell your mom or dad or teacher about the problem, too.

3. What is my plan?

Now you have discovered a lot of different things you might do to solve the problem. The next step is to select one—and of course, the best one. So ask yourself which "solution" you think will work best for YOU, one that is likely to make things better. For example, one way of solving the name-calling problem would be to tell that person that he or she has hurt your feelings, and to then ask the person to stop calling you names. Or maybe you select a different "plan." The important thing is to think through all the ways you could solve the problem, and select the best idea. In other words, think carefully before you decide what to do.

4. When will I do this?

Next, decide when you will carry out your plan. Will you do it today, or tomorrow, or next week?

5. How did my plan work?

After you have carried out your plan, think about what happened as a result. Did things work the way you wanted? If so, your problem is on its way to being solved. If not, what is the next best thing you can do? Who else did you tell your problem to?

OKAY, TIME TO PRACTICE!

Josh has a problem. Using this 5-Step process, help Josh solve his problem.

1. What is the problem?

"Danny called me 'stupid' and it made me upset."

2. How can I solve it?

✓ I could call him "stupid" right back.

✓ I could tell Danny to stop calling me names.

✓ I could tell Danny how upset it makes me and ask him to apologize.

✓ I could sit down and cry.

✓ I could share my candy bar with Danny, and hope that will get him to stop calling me "stupid."

✓ I could hit Danny.

✓ I could ignore Danny and hope he doesn't call me "stupid" again.

✓ I could ask Danny if he would like to be my friend.

What else could Josh do?

✳ _____

✳ _____

✳ _____

3. What is my plan?

I'll tell my mom about the problem, and tell her I'm going to tell Danny to stop calling me names.

4. When will I do this?

I'll tell my mom about this now. I'll tell my teacher about it at school tomorrow. I'll talk to Danny tomorrow at school during lunch.

5. How did my plan work?

My plan worked great. I said it politely. Danny said he was sorry. I think we can be friends. I told my teacher about it.

HELP SUSAN SOLVE HER PROBLEM

Susan has a problem. Using this 5-Step process, help Susan solve her problem.

1. What is the problem?

"My homework isn't done, and I have to leave for school in a few minutes."

2. How can I solve it?

✓ I could try to finish my homework on the way to school.

✓ I could ask my mom to help me right now and see if I can finish the homework before we go to school.

✓ I could tell my teacher a dragon ate my homework and that's why I can't turn it in.

✓ I could ask my friend if she would let me copy her homework.

✓ I could ask my mom if I could stay home from school today since my homework isn't done.

✓ When I get to school, I could ask the teacher if I could turn the assignment in tomorrow instead of today.

What else could Susan do?

✳ _____

✳ _____

3. What is my plan?

I will ask the teacher if I can turn the assignment in tomorrow instead of today. I will tell my mother all about my problem, too.

4. When will I do this?

I will ask my teacher when I get to school. I will talk to my mom and dad at dinner time this evening.

5. How did my plan work?

My plan worked great. My teacher said it would be okay to turn in my late homework tomorrow, but only this once. I am going to get my homework done on time from now on.

HELP CARLOS SOLVE HIS PROBLEM

Carlos has a problem. Using this 5-Step process, help Carlos solve his problem.

1. What is the problem?

"My brother takes my favorite toys without asking me."

2. How can I solve it?

✓ I could tell my brother he has to ask me if it is okay with me if he plays with my toys.

✓ I could tell my brother how upset I get when he takes my things, and ask him not to.

✓ I could yell at my brother for playing with my toys without asking me first.

✓ I could take his toys.

✓ I could ignore the problem and just be upset.

✓ I could hide my toys so my brother can't find them.

✓ I could show my brother which toys he could play with, and which ones he absolutely cannot touch.

What else could Carlos do?

✳ _____

✳ _____

✳ _____

3. What is my plan?

I'm going to show my brother which toys he can play with, and which ones he cannot play with. I will tell my parents all about it.

4. When will I do this?

I will do this now.

5. How did my plan work?

My plan worked great. My little brother liked that he has permission to play with some of my toys. He says he promises to not play with the toys I said he has to leave alone.

HELP SERENA SOLVE HER PROBLEM

Serena has a problem. Using this 5-Step process, help Serena solve her problem.

1. What is the problem?

Serena told her mom she did not have a spelling quiz tomorrow at school, but this is not the truth. Serena feels bad about not telling the truth.

2. How can I solve it?

✓ I could tell my mom the truth and say, "I'm sorry."

✓ I could study for my quiz now.

✓ I could ignore it and hope my mom never finds out.

What else could Serena do?

✳ _____

✳ _____

✳ _____

3. What is my plan?

I am going to tell my mom the truth and tell her that "I'm sorry" for not being truthful with her.

4. When will I do this?

I will do this right now.

5. How did my plan work?

My plan worked great. Mom said I showed courage to say "I'm sorry." She told me to always tell the truth.

Okay, it's your turn to practice solving problems of your own. Think of a problem you have. Use these 5-steps below to solve your problem.

1. What is my problem?

_____

_____

_____

2. How can I solve it?

_____

_____

_____

3. What is my plan? Who will I tell about my problem?

_____

_____

_____

4. When will I do this?

_____

_____

_____

5. How did I my plan work?

_____

_____

_____

PART II

DON'T MAKE A PROBLEM BIGGER THAN IT REALLY IS

Sometimes a problem looks bigger than it is, and that can be stressful. It also makes it more difficult to solve. It's important to not make the problem bigger than it is.

As you read about each of the children on the following pages, think of all the ways to help them think about their problems in the best way possible.

HELP TYRONE SOLVE HIS PROBLEM

1. What is the problem?

"School is very hard for me."

How can Tyrone think more clearly about the problem so it becomes easier to solve? Here is what Tyrone said.

2. How can I solve it?

I really like most of my subjects in school, but math is hard. I like to do additions and subtractions, but multiplications are difficult. I need to get more help with multiplications.

✓ I can ask my mom, or dad or my teacher to help me learn multiplications.

What else could Tyrone do?

✳ _____

✳ _____

✳ _____

3. What is my plan?

I will ask my mom and dad and my teacher to help me learn multiplications.

4. When will I do this?

I will ask mom and dad this evening when we have dinner. I will ask my teacher tomorrow at school right after the class.

5. How did my plan work?

My plan worked great. My parents have hired an older student to tutor me, and my teacher says I can stay after school for a few minutes for some extra help, too.

Maria is 9 years old. She is very tall for her age. She is taller than all the other children in her class. Courtney and Tiffany call her names like "beanpole" and "skyscraper."

Maria is very upset by all this and says to her mother, "None of the other kids like me."

Everyone wants to be liked, to have friends. It is no fun to feel that others don't like you, but is that really the problem? Is Maria making the problem bigger than it is?

1. What is the problem?

"No one likes me."

Maria thinks that none of the other children like her. But is that really true? Is Maria making the problem bigger than it is? To find out, Maria could ask herself questions like these:

- ▶ Is Courtney and Tiffany making fun of me, or just having fun but not intending to be "mean"?

- ▶ How do I feel about being called "beanpole" and "skyscraper?"

- ▶ Does my being called "beanpole" and "sky-scraper" mean ALL my classmates don't like me?

2. How can I solve it?

✓ I could tell Courtney and Tiffany they hurt my feelings when they call me "beanpole" and "skyscraper."

- ✓ I could tell my classmates I don't like to be called those names.
- ✓ I could ask Courtney and Tiffany if they would like to be friends.
- ✓ I could ignore Courtney and Tiffany.
- ✓ I could decide I don't need to be friends with Courtney and Tiffany.

3. What is my plan?

I am going to tell my teacher about the problem I am having with Courtney and Tiffany. I am going to tell Courtney and Tiffany that I don't like to be called "beanpole" and "skyscraper."

4. When will I do this?

I will tell my teacher about my problem at school tomorrow. I am going to talk to Courtney and Tiffany at recess tomorrow.

5. How did my plan work?

My plan worked great. Courtney and Tiffany said they wished they were as tall as I am and that being called "beanpole" and "skyscapper" is cute and not "bad." Courtney and Tiffany said they considered themselves my friends. I told them that I am now okay with being called "beanpole" and "skyscraper."

Edward had to give a book report in front of the class. "I don't like being up there all by myself," he said. "Everyone stares at me and it makes me nervous. I forget what I am going to say."

1. What is the problem?

"Everyone laughs at me when I talk in front of the class."

Edward was so upset he pretended to be sick. He stayed home the day he was supposed to give the report. When he went back to school, the teacher told him he would have to give the report anyway.

2. How can I solve it?

What can Edwards do to breakdown the problem in a way to help him solve it?

- ✓ I get nervous when I talk in front of the class, but so does almost everyone else.
- ✓ I know my classmates think of me as a friend so they are not going to laugh at me.
- ✓ I could stay home from school on the day of my report.
- ✓ I could tell my teacher I am not going to give my report.

3. What is my plan?

I will tell the teacher how nervous I feel when speaking in front of the class. I am going to give the report and know that my classmates sometimes get nervous when they get in front of the class, too.

4. When will I do this?

I will talk to my teacher when class begins. I will give the report tomorrow, as planned.

5. How did my plan work?

My plan worked great. I realized that everyone is a little worried and nervous speaking in front of the class. There is nothing to be ashamed of if you are nervous. I kept in mind that almost everyone in my class has the same feeling and that made things better.

When you feel too busy, you can get stressed and become upset and worried and unhappy. Brad is feeling this way.

Brad goes to school from 8:00 to 2:30 every weekday. He has soccer practice from 2:45 to 4:15 three days a week. When he gets home, around 4:30, he has to do his chores. Then he has dinner with his family. Then Brad does his homework, and then he goes to bed. He almost never gets to ride his bike with his friends these days. Brad is even busy on the weekends. He has a soccer game. He has homework. Brad also has to help take care of his younger brother when his mother goes grocery shopping. Brad feels as though he never has any time to do the things HE really wants to do. Help Brad solve his problem.

1. What is the problem?

"I am too busy. I don't have time to do all the things I want to do, and relax."

2. How can I solve the problem?

So that he could decide how to best solve his problem, he decided to write down what chores and responsibilities he had to do each day.

MORNING ACTIVITIES

✓ Wake up at 7:15
✓ Take a shower, brush teeth, wash face, brush my hair

✓ Make bed
✓ Get dressed for school
✓ Feed my dog Bonzo
✓ Have breakfast
✓ Help clear the dishes off the table
✓ Make sure homework and books are packed in my backpack
✓ Go to school

ACTIVITIES AT SCHOOL

✓ Go to Class#1
✓ Go to Class#2
✓ Have Lunch
✓ Go to Class #3
✓ Go to Class#4
✓ Go to Class#5

AFTER SCHOOL ACTIVITIES

✓ Feed and walk Bonzo, my dog
✓ Have a snack
✓ Go to soccer practice
✓ Do chores
✓ Have dinner
✓ Do homework
✓ Get ready for bed (take a shower, brush teeth)

After looking at his schedule Brad decided that everything on that list had to be done, but that he wanted a little bit more time for himself. He said, "I do like to be busy. It's fun. I like to do well in school, and that's why I study. I like to play soccer with my friends. I am proud that my parents think I am responsible. Maybe when I get home from school, I can rest and have a snack before I do my chores. That will make me feel better, and it will be time I have all for myself.

3. What is my plan?

When I get home from school, I will take a little time for a snack and watch my favorite tv show and then do homework and complete my chores. I will tell my parents that it seems to me that I don't have enough time to relax. I will plan to use my time wisely. This leaves me with more time for me.

4. When will do this?

I will talk to my parents at dinner time this evening.

5. How did my plan work?

My plan worked great. I now take some time for myself to relax so that I don't feel so overwhelmed.

How about you? Do you sometimes feel as if you are too busy? You have school during the day. You have homework at night. You have chores around the house. Your pet wants your attention and to play. Maybe you have piano lessons and soccer practice. You do a lot of things with your parents. Write down all the things you do each day.

MORNING ACTIVITIES

_____
_____
_____
_____
_____

AT SCHOOL

_____
_____
_____
_____
_____

AFTER SCHOOL ACTIVITIES

_____
_____
_____

_____

_____

_____

SPECIAL THINGS TO DO

_____

_____

_____

Using the 5-Step problem solving process, "solve" a problem you are having.

1. What is my problem?

_____

_____

2. How can I solve it?

_____

_____

3. What is my plan? Who will I tell about my problem?

_____

_____

4. When will I do this?

_____

_____

5. How did I my plan work?

_____

_____

PART III

OTHER THINGS YOU CAN DO THAT MAKE IT EASIER TO SOLVE PROBLEMS

You have been learning about how you can best solve problems, and not make them bigger than they are. Here are some other important ways that help you be your very best—which can help to better solve problems, too.

EXPRESS YOURSELF

Are you good at saying what you mean? Can you express yourself in a way that others understand what you are saying?

* Do you find it easy to talk with your parents and teachers?

* Can you ask others for what you need?

* Can you tell others how you feel?

✳ Do you tell others what you want and need?

Write your answers to the following questions. When you are done, read your answers out loud. Remember, think about how you feel and what you want and need.

1. A classmate asks to cut in front of you in the lunch line. What do you say?

_____

_____

_____

2. Your brother/sister wants to watch a special TV program. He/she walks over to change the channel. You want to watch the show you were watching. What do you say?

_____

_____

_____

3. A classmate asks to copy your homework for an assignment. You don't want to let him / her copy your work. What do you say?

_____

_____

_____

4. The teacher asks the entire class to stay after school because someone else was talking. You don't want to take the blame for something you didn't do. What do you say?

_____

_____

_____

5. A friend wants to borrow your favorite baseball cap. You are afraid the cap will get dirty, or lost. What do you

tell your friend?

_____

_____

_____

6. You are watching your favorite TV show that will end in ten minutes. Your dad or mom says you must turn it off immediately. What do you say to convince them to let you have 10 more minutes of television watching time?

_____

_____

_____

7. A schoolmate is being a bully to you. Who do you tell? What do you say?

_____

_____

_____

8. You don't understand a problem the teacher has just explained. What do you say to the teacher?

_____

_____

_____

It's very important that you learn positive ways to communicate. It can help you solve many problems, and even prevent some in the first place.

BEING YOUR OWN "BEST FRIEND"

It's really important to like yourself, to be your own best friend. Are you your own best friend? Write down 5 things that show you are a friend to yourself.

1. _____

_____

_____

2. _____

_____

_____

3. _____

_____

_____

4. _____

_____

_____

5. _____

_____

_____

GOOD SELF-ESTEEM HELPS YOU BE, AND DO, BETTER

What you think about yourself is called self-esteem. Your self-esteem is what you think of YOU.

Having a healthy self-esteem means that YOU like yourself. When you like yourself, you are going to treat yourself nicely, just as you do to a best friend.

When you like who you are, you are patient with yourself. You respect yourself.

What do you think "respect yourself" means?

_____

_____

_____

How you see yourself has a lot to do with how you act. If you see yourself as a good friend, you will "act" like a good friend. If you see yourself as a good student, you are going to "act" like a good student.

Your self-esteem is made up of the positive and negative thoughts and feelings you have about yourself. You might, for example, believe any of the below POSITIVE, or NEGATIVE, things about yourself. Draw a circle around those you believe about yourself.

Positive

- I'm smart.
- I'm fun.

- I'm a good friend.
- I learn from my mistakes.

Negative

- No one likes me.
- I'm not a good student.
- I'm too tall.
- I am too short.
- I'm not very good at doing things.

The more positive feelings you have about yourself, the better you will feel like a "can do" person!

And here's even more good news: It's not what others say about you, but rather, what YOU say to yourself about yourself that is most important.

Think positive. If you think of yourself as smart, you will speak in class and enjoy class more.

If you feel like a good friend, you will act that way. You will be a good friend.

What you think about yourself is very important. It can make your whole life better. Each morning look in the mirror and say, "Well hello there, good friend!" Try it. You can't say it without smiling. It's a good feeling to have a good friend!

List 5 things you liked about yourself, and why!

1. _____

_____

2. _____

_____

3. _____

4. _____

_____

5. _____

_____

What one thing could you do to feel even better about yourself?

_____

_____

_____

SHARING HAPPINESS

It is sometimes easy to tell people when we are unhappy. We must also tell them when we are happy.

When you are happy, it makes others feel happy, too.

Do you feel happy when you make someone a present? Are you happy when you cheer someone up?

Making others happy is a good thing, but so is doing things to make yourself happy.

1. Describe 3 things that make you feel happy.

✓ _____

✓ _____

✓ _____

2. Describe something you did that made someone else feel happy.

■ _____

_____

3. Think of someone who made you feel happy this week. What did that person do or say to make you feel happy?

✳ _____

_____

```
............................................
:                                          :
:          SHARING POSITIVE                :
:              FEELINGS                     :
:                                          :
............................................
```

It is always nice to have others share their positive feelings about you. Others like it when you share your postivie feelings towards them. Use sentences that start with these words to help you share your feelings:

✓ I appreciate you when . . . _____

_____

_____

✓ I liked it when you . . . _____

_____

_____

✓ It was really helpful when you . . . _____

_____

_____

What can you say to make your parents feel good? Start your sentence by using the words like the following.

✴ I liked it when you . . . _____

_____

✴ It was really helpful when you . . . _____

_____

✴ I appreciate it when you. . ._____

_____

Try this with grandparents, too. Try it with your friends. Try it with your teachers. You will see how well it works to make you feel better about yourself—and help solve your problems, too.

WHO IS YOUR "HELP! TEAM"?

It can be very comforting to know that others are on your side and willing to help you! We call this your "Help! Team." It can include your mom and dad, your siblings, and your grandparents, even your teachers, favorite aunts and uncles and best friends, too.

You know people who are eager to help you. Think about who they are. List five people.

✓ _____

✓ _____

✓ _____

✓ _____

Now pick a person who has helped you recently. What did he or she do to help? Here's what Jason wrote:

Jason's "Help! Team"

WHO: <u>My Dad</u>

WHAT: <u>Yesterday I forgot my lunch money. My dad brought it to me even though he had to leave work and drive to school.</u>

HOW: <u>Dad wasn't upset. He didn't feel I was "forgetful." He was concerned that I had lunch.</u>

MY "Help! Team"

Now it's your turn. Who supports you?

WHO: Name one person who helps you.

_____

_____

_____

WHAT: What does he or she do to help you?

_____

_____

_____

HOW: How does that person let you know that he or she cares about YOU?

_____

_____

_____

Isn't that a nice feeling? Now, try this exercise again. This time think about who YOU help.

How I Help Others

WHO: Name one person you are there for when they need you.

_____

WHAT: What do you do to show support for that person?

_____
_____

HOW: How do you let that person know that you support him or her when needed?

_____
_____

EAT FOODS THAT ARE GOOD FOR YOU

One of the most important things you can do is to take care of yourself. Yes, your parents take care of you. But, you have to help. Seeing that you get the nutrition you need to stay healthy is one of the most important things you can do.

You can follow three simple rules.

1. Eat breakfast. You may be in a rush in the morning. You may think you don't have time to eat breakfast. Breakfast is the fuel that gets your body and brain going. A good breakfast can keep you alert all day long. Not eating breakfast is like expecting your family's car to run without any gas.

2. <u>Eat the right foods</u>. Good food helps you grow, and think better. Too much junk food isn't good for your body and can make you nervous and grumpy.

3. <u>Eat enough food</u>. Because you are growing so rapidly, your body needs plenty of good food.

What else can you do to be sure you are eating foods that are good for you?

_____

_____

_____

EXERCISE IS IMPORTANT TO THINKING CLEARLY

Another way to take care of yourself is by getting enough exercise. Think about how good you feel after recess. You have more energy after playing with friends. You feel good when you are running and jumping around!

Exercise helps your blood takes more oxygen to the brain. You can think better. Exercise also strengthens your muscles and your bones. Exercise actually makes you LESS tired! Exercise makes you feel more energetic. When you are less tired, you feel happier.

What exercise do YOU like to do? List three things you enjoy (like riding your bike or swimming or playing fetch with your dog).

✻ _____

✻ _____

You probably spend a good amount of time sitting in class each day. This makes it even more important to get some exercise each day. Today you may take a walk with your mom or dad. Tomorrow you may play ball with your friends. The important thing is that you keep active. What else can you do to get enough exercise?

GOOD WAYS TO RELAX

Being your best also means you know how to RELAX when you need to! To relax is to slow down, to calm down, to unwind. There are several ways you can relax.

Deep Breathing: The Correct Way to Breath

Take a deep breath, as deep as you can. Really get a lot of air in you! As you let it out, can you feel yourself relaxing a little? By breathing deeply, you force yourself to slow down. You concentrate on one thing at a time. Whenever you feel that things are too much, take several deep breaths.

You can do this anywhere, anytime.

Here are the steps:

1. Sit down. Get comfortable.

2. Close your eyes.

3. Take a deep breath in, as deep as you can.

4. Let the breath out slowly.

5. Put your hands on your stomach and take another deep breath. Feel your stomach filling up with air.

6. Breathe out. Feel your stomach shrinking and letting the air out.

7. Do this several times.

8. Open your eyes.

9. Smile!
Don't you feel better and more relaxed?

Relaxing With Music

You can also relax with music. Choose a favorite soothing sound and lay back in your bed or sit in a comfortable chair. Think of nothing but the music.

Enjoy the sounds. Let the music fill your mind. Notice how you are relaxing.

Your muscles are relaxing. Your body feels better, too.

Relaxing is best with soothing music. The goal is to relax, not to become pumped up. Loud, energetic music will make you feel excited. Save that for those times when you want to be energetic.

Relaxing Your Muscles

When you are very busy, sometimes you get a headache and your muscles are tight. Has your neck ever felt stiff? You might tighten your jaw and rub your teeth together until your jaw aches. Your body tightens up. This can cause pain. You can stop the pain. The way to do this is called muscle relaxation.

You need to begin by concentrating on your muscles.

Look at your hands. Clench your fist as tightly as you can. Go ahead, make a tight fist, really tight.

Now slowly open your hand and shake it out. Notice how good that feels? Stare at your hand and try to relax it until it is limp. Next, think about the muscles in your jaw.

Open your mouth and let your jaw relax. Feel how comfortable that is.

Do the same for other muscles in your body. Concentrate on one area at a time Relax your feet, then your calves, then your thighs, all the way to the top of your head and the tips of your fingers. Once you get good at this exercise, you can do it almost automatically. When you feel too busy and your muscles are tightening, slow down and relax them.

You can do this exercise anywhere, even in your seat at school. All you need to do is think about the muscles and try to make them smooth.

❖ ❖ ❖

Okay, that's it for now. We hope all these things help you be your best, and, help you solve problems!

Again, be sure to tell your mom and dad or your favorite teachers about how your are doing.

Other Books by Bettie Youngs Book Publishers

Confidence & Self-Esteem for Teens

Jennifer L. Youngs

Confidence & Self-Esteem for Teens is about the ways that beauty manifests from within. Have you ever run across someone who looked pretty, but undid her beauty by the way she acted or treated others?

Compare that to someone who is thoughtful, confident and comfortable with herself and as a result, has a lovely presence about her.

This book shows you how to let your inner beauty shine through—things like the secrets of serenity, steps for staying cool under pressure, building your self-esteem, drawing security from loving others, setting goals and feeling purposeful—and more.

ISBN: 978-1-940784-35-9 • ePub: 978-1-940784-34-2

Health & Fitness for Teens

Jennifer L. Youngs

Health & Fitness for Teens covers a most essential topic for teens: having a healthy body, liking your body and being fit. It's also a time of constant change. We can feel like we're just getting to know who we are when suddenly we are someone totally different. This book uncovers some of the myths teens have for comparing themselves to a standard other than their own, and covers some very important ground on how to best take care of themselves so as to look and feel their very best.

ISBN: 978-1-940784-33-5• ePub: 978-1-940784-32-8

Law of Attraction for Teens

How to Get More of the Good Stuff, and Get Rid of the Bad Stuff!

Christopher Combates

Whether it's getting better grades, creating better relationships, getting into college, or attracting a special someone, the Law of Attraction works! Aligning goals with your intentions enables you to create a better life. Written for teens, this engaging book will help teens to set purposeful goals, and to think, act, andcommunicate in the most positive way possible.

ISBN: 978-1-936332-29-8• ePub: 978-1-936332-30-4

Lessons from the Gym For Young Adults

5 Secrets for Being in Control of Your Life

Chris Cucchiara

As a teen, Chris Cucchiara's life was a mess. Then he discovered the gym and he was transformed inside and out. Says Chris, "The gym taught me discipline, which led to achieving goals, which started a cycle of success." A much-admired high-performance coach for teens, in this book, Chris share his guiding principles on how to: develop mental toughness (a life without fear, stress, and anger); become and stay healthy and fit; build an "athlete for life" mentality that stresses excellence; and, set and achieve goals that matter.

ISBN: 978-1-936332-38-0 • ePub: 978-1-936332-34-2

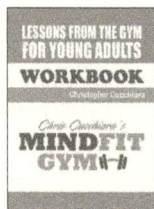

Lessons from the Gym For Young Adults

Workbook

Chris Cucchiara

A SUCCESS WORKBOOK FOR YOUNG ADULTS (ages 12-20) Do you lack self-confidence or have a difficult time making decisions? Do you sometimes wonder what is worth doing? Do you ever have a tough time feeling a sense of purpose and belonging? Chris shares his expertise of mastering success principles and shows you how to: Discover your real passion and purpose in life, which provides the drive, ambition and determination to overcome your limiting beliefs, fears, stress, and anger; Feel more in control of your life; Build your confidence and self-esteem; Build an athlete for life mentality that stresses leadership and excellence as a mindset; and, Stay motivated and set and achieve goals.

ISBN: 978-1-940784-16-8

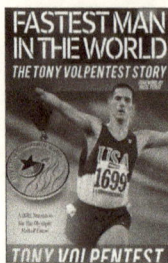

Fastest Man in the World
The Tony Volpentest Story

Tony Volpentest
Foreword by Ross Perot

Tony Volpentest, a four-time Paralympic gold medalist and five-time world champion sprinter, is a 2012 nominee for the Olympic Hall of Fame. This inspirational story details his being born without feet, to holding records as the fastest sprinter in the world.

"This inspiring story is about the thrill of victory to be sure—winning gold—but it is also a reminder about human potential: the willingness to push ourselves beyond the ledge of our own imagination. A powerfully inspirational story." **—Charlie Huebner, United States Olympic Committee**

ISBN: 978-1-940784-07-6 • ePub: 978-1-940784-08-3

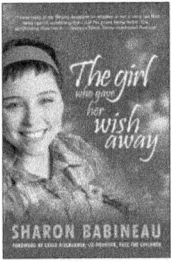

The Girl Who Gave Her Wish Away

Sharon Babineau
Foreword by Craig Kielburger

The Children's Wish Foundation approached lovely thirteen-year-old Maddison Babineau just after she received her cancer diagnosis. "You can have anything," they told her, "a Disney cruise? The chance to meet your favorite movie star? A five thousand dollar shopping spree?"

Maddie knew exactly what she wanted. She had recently been moved to tears after watching a television program about the plight of orphaned children. Maddie's wish? To ease the suffering of these children half-way across the world. Despite the ravishing cancer, she became an indefatigable fundraiser for "her children." In The Girl Who Gave Wish Away, her mother reveals Maddie's remarkable journey of providing hope and future to the village children who had filled her heart.

A special story, heartwarming and reassuring.

ISBN: 978-1-936332-96-0 • ePub: 978-1-936332-97-7

Red Dot
An Inspirational Short Story about a Remarkable Dog and the Children He Loved

Bettie J. Burres

Nothing compares to the faithfulness of the family dog. For six years Teddy has helped out on the family farm, walked the kids to the school bus, comforted them when they were sad, and snuggled with them through cold winter nights. In the dusk of a warm summer evening, when an intruder makes his way through the yard, threatening all that Teddy holds dear, the four children learn a devastating truth about the meaning of faithfulness.

A touching story of love—and ultimately, forgiveness.

ISBN: 978-1-936332-66-3• ePub: 978-1-936332-73-1

Abuconodozor
A Cat with An Attitude

John Rixey Moore

A darling and memorable cat story about a "not at-all-a-cat-person" who comes home one day to find that a stray Abssinian cat has decided to take up residency in his home. Reluctantly, he feeds the cat, and allows the cat to sleep on his bed. He begins to adore the cat, and comes to admire and respect her regal qualities, eventually naming the cat for an Abyssinian pharaoh, Abucodonozor. But the cat has a different idea.

ISBN: 978-1-940784-13-7 • ePub: 978-1-936332-89-2

Healthy Family, Happy Life
What Healthy Families Learn from Healthy Moms

Donna Schuller

Family, Health, Fitness & Nutrition expert Donna Schuller offers advice for improving health and wellness including the benefits the and paybacks of being honest with others; how wellness thoughts contribute to your being healthy; the significance of loving others and the imperative of loving oneself of exercise, sleep and happiness; how to get through hard times; how dietary supplementation work; the importance of nutrition, and more.

ISBN: 978-1-940784-11-3 • ePub: 978-1-940784-31-1

Flowers for Grandmother

Kendahl Brooke Youngs

Kendahl is looking forward to visiting her grandmother, and wants to surprise her with a present for her flower garden. When Kendahl and her mother go the local garden store, Kendahl sees a picture of a gladiola and tells her mother that that's what they should get for her Grandmother. Told to choose five bulbs, Kendahl picks what she thinks are five different colored gladiola bulbs—but she's in for a surprise.

Flowers for Grandmother is a charming story that not only reminds us of the special love between Grandparents and grandchildren, and nurtures that love and bonding. And, this lovely little book tickles that special funny-bone in children...teaching that not everything is what it appears to be, but also that when it comes to gift-giving, it's the thought that counts most. Fresh from the mega-best-selling "KENDAHL GETS A PUPPY," Kendahl's pup "Apple" has a special appearance in this delightful book for children and their grandparents.

ISBN: 978-0-9836045-7-0 • ePub:978-1-936332-12-0

Kendahl Gets a Puppy

Kendahl Brooke Youngs

Every year on her birthday, Kendahl has the same wish: she wants a puppy of her own. But every year, her mother tells her, "When you are older," reminding her that owning a puppy is a big responsibility—and a lot of work.

Finally, on her sixth birthday, Kendahl gets her wish. Her mom surprises her with a new puppy, whom Kendahl names "Apple." Though Kendahl is thrilled to finally have her cherished dog, Apple teaches her that owning a real puppy is not like having a stuffed animal. In this heartwarming illustrated story, a young girl learns that growing up is about more than the number of candles on your birthday cake; it is also about work, responsibility and unconditional love.

ISBN: 978-0-9836045-8-7 • ePub: 978-0-9836045-9-4

Toby, the Pet Therapy Dog and His Hospital Friends

Charmaine Hammond

Toby is a big, brown, happy dog. Every week, his owner, Miss Charmaine takes him to visit and comfort children who are in the hospital. Follow Toby the service dog for a day, and see how he makes friends with the children, helps make them happy.

* Beautifully illustrated, Toby, the pet Therapy Dog teaches young readers the wonders of being of service to others.

* A simple, happy story that also sends a positive message about community, as well as the importance of kindness to pets.

ISBN: 978-0-9836045-0-1• ePub: 978-0-9836045-1-8

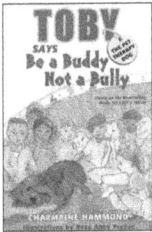

Toby, the Pet Therapy Dog Says Be a Buddy, Not a Bully

Charmaine Hammond

When Toby steps into the path of a dog who bullies him and shreds his beloved stuffed teddy-bear toy, we see the hurt feelings it creates. This beautifully illustrated book teaches children about the importance of kindness, respect, acceptance and being considerate of others, including pets. A wonderful story to start discussions in ages 3 to 10.

ISBN: 978-0-9836045-5-6 • ePub: 978-1-936332-31-1

I Have a Restaurant

Ryan Afromsky

What goes on behind the scenes after an order is placed? Where does the food come from? What does it look like "back there"? How does it all work?

In this popular children's book, Ryan, the restaurant owner, is your child's guide to learning everything that goes on in a restaurant, from the time the restaurant opens and gets ready to serve its customers, to taking a person's order and preparing it, to when the food arrives.

From opening to closing time, children will have fun and their curiosity will be sparked as they explore and learn about what happens behind the scenes of eating in a restaurant. Informative and amusing, with a diverse, colorful cast of characters,

I Have a Restaurant is a great way to educate and inspire kids, ages 3-7, about the lively teamwork and steps it takes to prepare and serve customers delicious meals.

ISBN: 978-0-9836045-2-5 • ePub: 978-0-9836045-3-2

FOR MORE READING
VISIT OUR WEBSITE AT:
www.BettieYoungsBooks.com

www.ingramcontent.com/pod-product-compliance
Lightning Source LLC
LaVergne TN
LVHW011414080426
835511LV00005B/530